Welcome to Groovy Kids' Body Language!   The following pages illustrate some body positions, movement and gestures that people use when interacting. You might notice some of these gestures when you watch people carefully.

You can try out these gestures to help you communicate with others. Words tell others about our thoughts and ideas. We can use feeling words to describe our emotions. Facial expressions and body language help others to see our feelings more clearly. Gestures make communicating more fun. They also help others understand us more fully.

You should try to be aware of other people's feelings when you talk to them. You can be a better friend if you understand how your behavior affects other people.

Personal space is an important part of body language. The smallest circle shows the boy's personal space. Another person can come into this zone only if the boy wants a hug or a friendly touch from someone he knows well.

The second circle shows places that the boy may want to move very suddenly. He may step to the side or move his arms. Most often we stand outside of this circle to talk to someone. This allows us to see each other's faces and feel comfortable.

The largest circle is the farthest from the boy. Outside of this is the social zone. People may walk by the boy outside this circle without disturbing him.

Try to leave space between yourself and others. Some places are crowded and there is not much space. This may happen in an elevator, bus or subway. Try not to touch other people. If people have to touch, they try to let only their arms touch each other.

Where is the best place to sit if these people are all strangers? Where do you sit if the curly haired boy is your friend?

If you are with the boy, sit next to him. If he is a stranger, leave at least one empty seat between you and him.

Use eye contact. Watch the person's eyes, eyebrows, mouth and nose to see his feelings.
What kind of information do these features tell you?

Do people's hair, ears, chin and forehead give you this information? Probably not. Try to focus on the most important features that can move and express feelings.

When you sit up straight and look directly at others, you seem confident. See the girl on the right using these techniques. Slouching, looking down and feet turned in make the first girl appear shy, sad or not confident. Look at yourself in the mirror when you are sitting. Try out the confident way of sitting.

A firm handshake shows confidence. Handshakes are used when meeting someone new, greeting in a formal setting or making a deal.

A weak handshake does not feel good to the other person. It lacks confidence and shows weakness.

Standing tall and keeping your head up shows confidence and friendliness. Leaning over and looking down do not.

A hand held high is used when greeting or saying goodbye to someone far away. It also can be a signal that you want to talk.

A hand held at eye level is for greeting someone near you. It can be used to signal that you want to talk in a small group of people. Both gestures can also be used to vote.

1. up   2. back down

This gesture uses movement to "flash" the eyebrows at someone. The eyebrows rise up and go back down quickly. The smile may get bigger for a second too. It means "Hello" to someone familiar.

This boy's arms are closed over his chest. He may not be feeling very friendly right now.

This girl's arms are behind or on the side of her body. This shows open, friendly mood.

This boy's arms are wide open and reaching. This means he wants a hug and is feeling very friendly.

Sometimes, a slight difference in the placement of someone's hand can make a huge difference in the meaning.

A hand holding the chin means that the person is thinking or deciding about something.

A hand clutching the throat means that the person is probably choking on something.

The arrows in this picture show the movement of her fingers. She is making a zipping gesture across her lips. It means "I won't tell the secret."

Cheering!

I did it!

Victory!

These three kids have their arms up. Each movement means "Hurray!" but each is a little different.

These two arm movements mean different things.

The boys are showing off their muscles. This means "I am strong." or "I can lift that".

The girl is pumping her fist in the air. It does not mean strength. It is a way to cheer for yourself, your team or your friend.

Hands up with elbows bent = "I give up!" This can be when police say "hands up". It can also be used if someone gives up during a sport or game. It means "I give up, you beat me."

Arms up with elbows straight = "I win" or "I did it!" This can be when someone scores points or does well in a sport.

Notice the difference in the elbows and the facial expressions.

A pat on the back means "good job". I can also mean "you can do it!"

Patting your own back is usually a joke. It means "I did a good job and I'm not going to wait for someone else to say so".

Thumbs up can mean "yes", "I like it.", "Good job!", "Go for it!" or "I'm o.k."

Thumbs down can mean "no", I don't like it.". "Don't do it." or "Things are not going well."

The girl is making an "O" with her fingers. It means, "O.k." We use this when we want to signal "I'm o.k.", "It's correct." or "Everything is good right now."

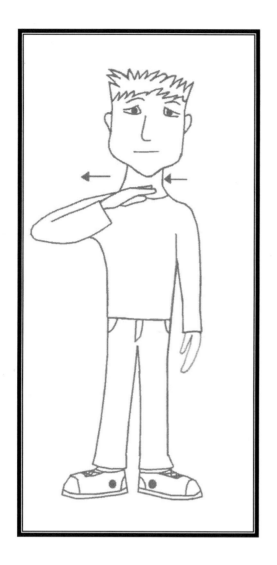 

Using a sawing motion back and forth across the neck means "stop".

Both hands in front are blocking her body. It is a signal to stop.

Hands over ears or fingers in ears = It's too loud...or
I don't want to hear what you're saying.

Biting finger = nervous

Blowing 1st finger = sh!

Hand in front =don't want to tell the truth

Finger in front of the mouth can mean different things. Look carefully at how these boys are placing their fingers.

Here's another example of fingers in mouth that means she's nervous. Biting nails shows that you are not sure of yourself.

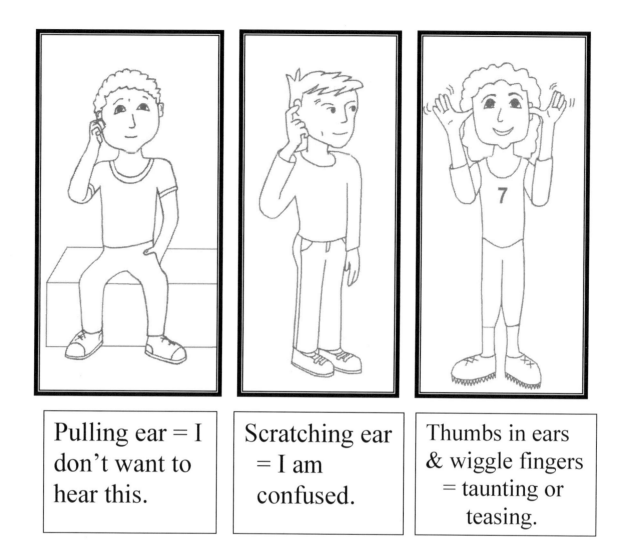

| Pulling ear = I don't want to hear this. | Scratching ear = I am confused. | Thumbs in ears & wiggle fingers = taunting or teasing. |

Look closely to these three pictures. Each person is touching their ears, but they are each a little different. The type of movement tells the meaning.

Here's another example of a finger movement near the ear. This time he is drawing an imaginary circle around his ear. It means "That's crazy!"

The boy who is sitting focuses his attention on his work. He shields his eyes from others by putting his hands on the sides of his head. This means "Do not disturb me."

This boy has closed his whole body up into a ball.
He does not want anyone to bother him.
This closed position can also mean "I can't take any more sadness. I'm so depressed."

This picture shows the boy licking his finger and then drawing an imaginary number 1 in the air. It means "I did something great!" It is like a joke, "I score one point!"

This boy is showing off too. He blows on his fingernails and then shines them on his shirt. It means "I did something very impressive."

The girl's eyelids are drooping and she holds her head up with her hand. It means "I'm bored."

The bottom picture shows a girl tapping her fingers on the table. It also means "I'm bored" or "I'm impatient."

These two kids are sticking their lower lip out. It is a "pout".

The boy shows angry eyes and closed fists. He is upset that he did not get his way.

The girl shows sad eyes and closed arms. She is sad and wants sympathy.

The girl is scratching her head. That is a sign that she is confused.

The boy has raised one eyebrow. This can mean that he is confused about what someone has said.

It may also mean that he thinks they did or said something weird.

 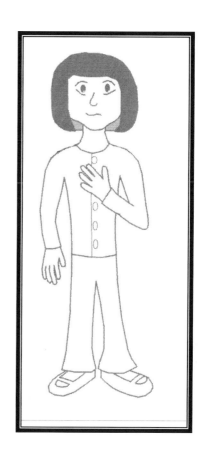

The first girl has raised both shoulders at the same time. This is called "shrugging" your shoulders. This gesture may have hands raised at the same time. It means "I don't know." It can also mean "I don't care."

The second girl places her hand on her own chest. Also, her eyes are open very wide. This is a gesture that means "Are you talking to me?"

The girl is drawing an imaginary "X" over her left side of her chest. This is where your heart is. The gesture is called "Cross my heart". It means "I promise."

This girl crosses two of her fingers in front of her body. The gesture is called "fingers crossed". It means "I hope so" or "good luck".

The boy crosses his fingers behind his back. He is hiding the gesture so the girl cannot see it. He shakes his head to mean "yes", but the hidden gesture means "no." He is lying to the girl.

Angry gestures are not appropriate unless the other person can clearly see that you are joking. Angry gestures suggest that you want to fight.

It is best to use words to say, "That makes me angry."

Some facial expressions are difficult to figure out. This is true when the eyes and mouth do not match.

This boy is smiling with his mouth, but his eyes and eyebrows say that he is angry. When the eyes and mouth do not match, look at the eyes to decide how they are really feeling! This boy is angry, but he wants to fool you. He may be planning something that is not nice.

This boy is smiling, but his eyes don't match. He's trying to say it's o.k., but inside he really feels worried or sad.

The last boy's smile is trying to cover up his feeling of confusion. He doesn't understand but doesn't want others to know that.

The first girl is sticking out her tongue at someone.
Some people do this when the other person is not
looking.

Sticking out your tongue means "I'm mad at you."
Sometimes little kids do this. It is very rude. Watch
out! You might get in trouble if you do this.

Jutting your chin at someone means "I'm mad at
you!" It is a childish way to express angry feelings.
Big kids and grown-ups learn to use words to say "I
don't like that."

The boy's face looks angry. He puts his hand behind his neck. This usually means "I'm feeling frustrated." People often put their hand behind their neck without knowing that they are doing it.

Tapping the side of your head can mean "I'm thinking." It can also mean "Use your brain."

Slapping the side of your head or forehead means "Oh yeah, I forgot!" It can also mean "Oh, I should have known that!

Hands in fists on the hips means "Hey, what are you doing?" It is used by someone in charge when others misbehave.

Hands open on hips means "I'm checking out what's going on." Some people do this when they enter a social situation to figure out what's happening and who they want to join.

Beating your chest means "I can do it" or "I'm strong". It is a gesture that imitates the strong gorilla.

When you slip your thumb quickly from touching the middle finger to the first finger, it makes a "snap" sound. Snapping can mean many things.

This boy snaps to get his dog's attention. Snapping to get a person's attention is considered rude.

Sometimes people snap to the beat of music, usually when they are happy.

If you hear someone say, "It's a snap!" This means "It's easy!" They may snap their fingers to show how fast the job can be done.

Rubbing your thumb quickly across your fingers means "I'm talking about money". Sometimes people use this gesture when something is expensive.

Pointing your finger at something means "look at this." Pointing in a general direction may mean "go this way."

This girl has her hands turned upward on her knees while she relaxes. Her eyes are closed so she can rest them. This body position is used as a relaxation strategy. It also can be used as a quick gesture to refer to relaxing or staying calm.

This girl kisses her fingers and then blows the imaginary kiss to someone she loves. This gesture means "I love you." It can be used when you are too far away for a hug. It also can be used to say, "Goodbye! I love you."

Now that you have learned a few new movements and their meanings, watch more closely when you talk to people to see what they are really saying.

Try a few gestures out in front of the mirror. How do they look?

Remember to always try to be polite to others and use your words to express your angry feelings.

Use a confident posture and you will notice people will respect you more. You may even start to feel more confident.

Have fun and use a sense of humor! See what happens when you smile more often. You just might find everyone smiling back at you!

Made in the USA
Charleston, SC
09 September 2013